Words Of Honey

Raw Honey

By

The Poetic Yogi

Blank Canvas

This clear blank canvas provides me

An opportunity

To create whoever I want to be

I'm not quite sure when it happened

But y'all...

I lost my identity

You see...

My biggest accomplishment being a mother of four

Shows my task requires more

A mother at seventeen

Caused me to put the fun on hold

Cause now I have this little life to mold

A wife at twenty-five

Everything surrounded around my guys

All five

As the boys began to grow

The world opened up

And showed me something I didn't know existed

I began to see my purpose

I started being a mother and wife

But there was more in store for this life

The blank canvas was uncovered through The Dirt

Showing me the opportunity

To grow...develop...becoming what only my wildest dreams could see

This blank canvas is the freedom to JUST BE!

Just Be Me!

Being whoever I want to be

Unapologetically

I'm not sure exactly when it happened

But y'all...

I lost my identity

I lost what I thought was me

I used this blank canvas to reinvent me

Now I'm the ME

I'm purposed to be

Sweet

Unique

Chocolate

HONEEEYYY

I Choose Me

I thought I wanted you

But I really wanted me

I thought I wanted to love you unconditionally

Be excited for you when you couldn't be

Lending my love...loyalty...and breath to thee

I wanted to share all of me with you

From the excitement of my pleasures...my joy

To the sorrows of my pain

But then I realized

I need to share all of me with me wholeheartedly

No matter what the circumstances may be

I gotta love me unconditionally

This rare vessel has been shattered with
grief...disappointment and despair

No...don't be sad

The way this heart is set up

It will always prevail

This heart belong to

THE ONE

The one who is love and the creator of love

When I call on him

My pain withers away

My heart aches no more

So yeah...

I thought I wanted you

Then I realized

I CHOOSE ME!!!

I choose the excitement of all my pleasures

All my joy

All my pain

They are FOR ME

Not to unload on any

But for me to stand in my purpose

Celebrating my individuality

As the sweet...

Unique...

POETIC YOGI

Mended Heart

It's a different kind of strength when you gotta mend your heart

I had to get real with me

Letting me know that I am worth more than what I settle for

It's time to heal my own heart

What I thought was for me

Continues to hurt me

Because it's not for me

It's time to reach in the fibers of my own heart space

Deep into the vessels that pump blood for breath

The vessels that ache from the twisted thoughts

The hurtful words

The deceptive deeds

It's time to hug myself through the pain

Telling me I will be alright

Today is a better day

And I'm all I got

I have felt alone

Even in the sea of many

Feeling my heart break

The blood dried in the stiffen broken areas

Just the thought breaks your heart

Takes your breath away

My heart is shielded by the rib God made just for you

That very rib

Promised to cherish...love...and protect me

Instead...

It was grabbed, yanked, shook up, and dropped

Damn...

You dropped my heart

My fault he says

He didn't realize he had it

I guess he didn't

When the other hearts he juggled

Taking priority over mine

Mine no longer mattered

It was too pure

Too sweet

Too full of love

You would rather have the heart full of hate

Than the one full of love

The one you're comfortable with

I love you today

But not tomorrow

Well I hate to disappoint you

But my love isn't set up like that

So you chose to break my heart

Because my love was too much for you

But don't worry about me

I will heal my own heart

I will mend my own scars

I will prevail

My vessels will return

And my blood will start to flow

My heart will generate in places you tried to incinerate

But don't worry about me

Because one thing for sure

I will mend my own heart

Questions

Am I just a phone call to pass the time?

Am I the one you say she's mine?

Do you truly care about my day?

Maybe you would rather hear me say the words the way I
say

Does that brighten your day?

Is there something you secretly have in store?

When will you trust me to tell me more?

Do you want to build a foundation to create our dreams?

Maybe you just want to do your own thang?

So many questions running through my mind

Taking me through this love whirlwind

Having my heart on a mission

Without permission

A mission to connect with you

Build with you

Lay with you

Enjoy every moment with you

This is my mission

I want to be true to you

Spend my life with you

But is your mission to engulf me too?

Some days you want me

Other days you don't know me

And even when you don't want me

Those are the days I want you even more

Yearning for something more

But you see...

The love I have for you

Has no conditions

It gets deeper and deeper than the day before

Because you are my soul connection

Who am I to you?

When you are my everything

Drop your guard

Open up your door

Allow our connection to grow even more

For I am your best friend

Your angel

Your confidante

Your co-defendant

And so much more

All I want is for us to soar and explore

But the questions that arise

Makes me question the unanswered questions

But maybe the answer is to stop questioning

Drop the expectations

And erase the disappointments

So many questions you really don't want the answer to

Thinking it's like this

When it's really like that

Just stop it

It's time to straighten your crown of peace

Pull together that cloak of joy

Embrace the now

Receive the love

Drop the questions

And just have fun

Don't worry about the questions or the answers

When you live in a place of anticipation

Of miraculous situations

When you live in a place that makes you awe God's beauty

The only question you should have is...

Wow... Lord is this all for me?

Then you hear that soft still voice

Saying to you

Yes child...it's all for you to question no more

Surrender

I surrender my heart...my pain...my love...my disdain

I surrender to be your Queen

I surrender...accept...and receive everything

My soul is here

Ready to connect with the soul of my king

Ready to ignite and create the twin flames of the soul

My spirit surrendered to his

His spirit connected to mine

Our spirit reigning in power

The same spirit showering of love

I surrender my love

To prepare and open

An abundance of love

My king will pour into me

That kinda love I can't imagine

That kinda love that reaches my heart

The part that's never beaten

I surrender to love

Ready to be the Queen God created me to be

I am his safe place

I am everything he needs me to be

Today...I surrender all of me

My pride...my dominance...my independence

Today I surrender my heart to thee

Ready to feel and be fully filled by my king

I am yours

Take me

Help me

Guide me

Love me

Today...I surrender all of me to all of you

The Heart Speaks

Speak with your heart and not your lips

Allow me to hear your heartfelt thoughts

Listen to your words

The rhythm of your heartbeat

How sweet the music is

Your heart beats in rhythm

For my love to sing

Speak with your heart

I will hear you every time

Your thoughts are loud when said from the heart

I hear them clearly

You say things from your heart

Things your lips will never speak

I hear you say

I love you and everything about you

I listen for your heart's echo

The one that repeats its love for me

Over and over again

Your heart said it

My heart felt it

Your mind infused in it

My body relaxed in it

As your face smiles to it

Your heart starts to love

As our bodies follows it

Thinking love was hard

But you finally opened your heart

And gave love a try

It's time to live...love...and be loved

Say it with your heart

Less with your lips

I will always hear your heartfelt thoughts

Speaking to me in ways I can't describe

I hear you

I feel you

I'm nowhere near you

We haven't talked in days

But we talk constantly

I hear your heart

You feel mine

I feel our love combined

The way our hearts speak to each other

Is like no other

This heart language we speak

Only we can comprehend

Our two-way communication

Allowing our mouths to rest

And our lips not to part

We have a heartfelt language

For us...by us...

Letting our heart speak as one

Hidden Love

Your heart is hidden

Stowed away hoping not to be found

Then one day

There she stands

And something special happens

Your heart beats calmly

Every time she's near

Not the constant pattern of fear

Your love revealing itself

Is it true?

Did your heart unearth the pain?

Did your love reach through the disdain...feeling the rain?

Did your heart feel love?

What is this?

It must've come from above

Unearthing the pain

Feeling your heart again

Who is she?

What has she done?

Why does she love you?

Why does she want you?

Doesn't she see you're Mr. Wrong?

When she deserves Mr. Right?

But she wants you

Wanting to love you unconditionally

Never thinking you would ever find the one

Someone who wants only you

Someone who knows how to love you so sweetly

So gently

So genuinely

Who is she?

She is me

The one who knows how to speak to your hidden heart

Connections

Connections are undeniable

Attractions are indescribable

Inner G...always reliable

It's the force that keeps us together

Thousands of miles apart

That telepathic connection

Making our hearts speak

Uttering no words

It has no sound

Our connection is undeniable

Attraction is indescribable

This love speaks soul to soul

It's beyond what man knows

Transcending space

Getting lost in time

This love has power

This love is full

This love is more than powerful

It's undeniable

Indescribable

Always reliable

1992 to 2017

1992 to 2017

My body only knew you

That's not how you perceived it to be true

Accusing me of lusting with every Tom, Henry, and Harry

Damn...even the Wal-Mart greeter?

Your thoughts of me

Laced with disloyalty and deceitfulness

But deep down

You know that shit isn't true

I gave you four sons

Doesn't that even matter?

Not even a little bit?

I know you love your boys with everything you got

So why do you choose to tear their mother down the way you do?

1992 to 2017

My everything belonged to you

Giving up everything

Just to be next to you

The love we shared is a guide

Representing black love

Showing what teamwork is between two

You chose to love me

The same way your mother loved you

Unsure love

Love wrapped in conditions

Laden with expectations

How could this be a healthy relationship with the mother
of your children?

I can see now how it was hard for you to love me

The way I loved you

So effortlessly

I don't knock it

I know your love was true

I know you did everything you could do

The pain engulfed in your life wasn't your fault

It was hard to navigate this part

When that little boy was screaming for someone to hold
his heart

When I came along at the age of sixteen

I know it felt like a dream

Because it was a dream to me too

Sixteen and right off of Vincennes

I had no idea the Dixon legacy had just begun

Having no idea I was meeting my husband

Four kids...two dogs...a rabbit...and a hamster later

Who would've known?

We would have a divorce too

Not because we don't love one another

But there was too much toxicity

Making our pain grow

Until it explodes

What was one...has now become two

Two lives to separate

Two lives healing the pain

Decreasing the levels of toxicity too

The love we shared

Started in 1992

Although we divorced in 2015

I still wanted to be with you

The same way you wanted me too

Heading to H-Town in 2016

Things rapidly changed

My life needed a new scene

You shortly moved after that

In 2017 you met a new boo

But I still thought it could be me and you

Thinking our love will stand the test of time

Because our love is true

But reality kicked in

I suddenly realized

There was no more me and you

You were in love with your new boo

And I had to find me something new

Someone else for me to do

Since it was quite obvious

Our lovemaking time had expired

1992 to 2017

I only made love to you

You were the only one for me

Although you never thought it was true

One year before your death

The truth came out

You knew that I only had love for you

But the whole time

You chose to feed yourself lies

Which you knew hurt me to my core

To the point I had to throw up my hands

I couldn't do no more

One month before you died

You confessed your love to me

Saying how you love me and mad at you

For allowing your pride to get in the way

Stealing something great

Standing in the way of you living your best life

Although you're not here

I want you to know

From 1992 to 2017

I only had love for you

Watcher of Me

I set an alarm to wake up

To watch you sleep

Watch your breath move like sweet music through your body

Watching the rise and fall of your chest

Humming to the beat of each breath you take

Your eyes flutter as though you're dreaming of me

Watching as you sleep

Tossing a hand over there

And a foot over there

Ooooohhhhhh....

I see you don't have on any underwear

The thickness of your thighs

The marks of beauty stretched across your stomach

They are the map guiding me along the beaten path

Showing my love for you

I set an alarm

Just to wake up and watch you sleep

Kicking that one foot from under the sheet

Looking at your face

So peacefully asleep

Studying every inch of you

The curve of your brow

The length of your lash

The softness of your nose

The suppleness of your lips

I can't resist

Kissing you softly as you sleep

Doing my best not to wake you

Making you dream about kissing me

I set my alarm to wake up

And watch you sleep

But I cannot sleep

If my dreams aren't you

I'd rather wake up and watch you sleep

Then to not dream about you

Outcome

I love the woman I fought to become

So many days...

I was unsure of the outcome

So many moments...

My lens was covered with debris of unworthiness

Shame...

Guilt...

Mind laced with lies of discontentment

So many days...

I prayed to receive discernment

Ready to release this doubt

Ready to forgive and forget

This pain I've been holding for so long

I prayed for restoration

Hoping for something new

Well today I'm here to tell you

God delivered in a big way

In only a way that He can do

So this place I live today

Is nothing like yesterday

Every day I open my eyes

I give God thanks

For blessing me more than I could have ever hoped for

When I say blessings

I'm not talking about material things

I'm speaking of the unsurpassable joy

Unspeakable peace

This love in my heart is overflowing

Overflowing with gratefulness

For all God has bestowed upon me

I now understand

I was created as a woman of purpose

A woman of substance

So here I stand

In honor of my ancestors prayers

I've been through the fire

Coming out on the other side

Without a singe

Higher than I've ever been

So yes...

I love the woman I fought to become

Blessed with all these blessings reigning down upon me

Because in this season

I'm winning

And that's the outcome

Where's My Man

Where's my man?

I think he's in another country

But hopefully he's on this earth

Somewhere waiting for me

Ready to rock my world

But I don't think he's in Texas

Although...

This one time I thought he was

Oh yeah...

Another time too

But they weren't the man for me

The man who was for me

Had my heart from sixteen to forty-two

And as quiet as it's kept

He still has a piece of it

R.I.P. Choc G

You were my husband

And the boys and I miss you much

After our love fizzled away

I tried to get on this dating scene

It was too many clowns

They had no idea

How I do what I do

But then this one came along

And I thought we had a connection

But I found out very quickly

You can love someone

Who doesn't love you

Now I'm lead to believe

The guy for me

Is beyond the borders

Waiting to cross into the heartland of ME

He's anticipating the essence of my presence

Gazing at my eyes

Looking deep into my soul

Doing everything he can

To make us whole

United as one

In fact…

I'm sure my man's waiting under a tree

Grounded in his essence

Patiently waiting for me

 Life

Life will show you a thing or two

Requiring obligations you weren't ready to do

Making you pursue happiness

Ensuing the chase

When the truth lies inside of you

Showing you who you should be

Of course life will test you

Testing your stamina

Giving you strength to pursue your purpose

The purpose God put inside of you

You see...

We are made in a way

Unique and sweet individually

We're put here to show each other

How to use the dirt to grow

Showing each other the love of God

Purposed us for

New Love

New love is free of drama

Heavy on the let us just be

Love that is loyal and true

But your clarity isn't required

The crystal ball is clear

It's real

This new love is different

From the bond we share

The way you hold me in your thought

Professing...providing...and protecting my heart

Only with the utmost care

I see the love you have for me

Watching your eyes dance to the rhythm of my laugh

Sparkling at the shine of my smile

The way you love me

Shows in your tone

Soft yet stern

Making sure my heart and mind don't take a wrong turn

Loving me skillfully

Intentionally with focus

Quality of accuracy

Like Picasso creating his masterpiece

Our love is the master

Giving us undeniable and indescribable peace

You have unlocked this heart

After seeing my pain

Choosing to learn what hurt me

Making sure I don't hurt like that again

Thank you for choosing me

Choosing to love me

Choosing to show me a better way

Making me laugh

At the drop of a dime

I love the way you love me

The way your hands rub on me

Memorizing every piece of me

Feeling my curves

My lines

My bumps and bruises

Your fingers exploring

Learning every piece of me

Returning the love in each touch

Each kiss

Each word you say

The love you pour in each cell

Overwhelming my heart

Understanding the roles we play

Keeping what we got strong

With happiness and communication

With consistency

You see...

It's not about making each other happy

When we're already there individually

For us...

It's about being together

Combining a happiness of two

As we become a powerful one

That's the power we hold

When we are strong in loyalty

And our love ain't blind

It was made from above

God molded us to be

We are the symbol of what faith

Wrapped in patience can become

A love that lasts for many forever's

A love that is new

A love that is true

A love that is rare

Hey Sis

Have you ever talked to a black woman?

Did you inquire about her cares?

Saving her from her fears

Or did you add to her tears?

Did you let her know her tears need not be considered a fear?

Did you tell her that being strong for too long will leave you feeling hollow...aching...and alone?

Yeah...I didn't think you told her

It's cool though

We all have our shit to deal with

Hey Sis...

Hear me out

I know what we go through day in and out

Having to do a little bit more to prove what we're about

Why we gotta grind harder?

Why we take so much pride in the grind

Can't we handle our business with a grin?

And remain feminine

We can do BOTH

We can DO IT ALL

We are light

The love

And the way

Our pure existence is what made every person who they are

Each and every day

WE BIRTH NATIONS

The power we hold is untold

Our look

Can make the biggest muthafucka fold

So Hey sis...

We gonna walk our walk

The way our Grandma's and Granny's taught us

We gonna talk our talk

Any damn way we please

Cause it's our voice

That's the change we need

We're gonna stand with our head held high

Fuck all that ride or die shit

It's time to create this space

Taking over this place

Like only Queens can do

They like to underestimate us

Thinking we're brand new

Let's show them

How we do what we do

Working quietly

Confidently

Allowing the volume of our work to scream through

So Hey Sis...

Today is all about us

Forget what folks said and done back in the day

We gotta let that shit go

It's poisonous anyway

It's time to stand in our purpose

Celebrating our individuality

In that sweet... unique

Chocolate Honey kinda way

Sippin' Tea...Writing Poetry

Sippin' something hot invokes thought

Feeling the warm liquid running through me

Giving me a new perspective

A fresh ability

Sippin' tea...writing poetry on a Sunday afternoon

It doesn't get any better than this

Especially when the words flow so effortlessly

Sippin' tea

Thinkin of all the words collectively

Creating this beautiful color maze

Known as my poetry

Clutching the cup

Feeling the heat

The warmness in my mouth

Making me think of what this mouth can do

What my mouth can be

As it sips on this hot cup of tea

Can my mouth bring my tongue to wrap words like poetry?

Will the words pulsate?

Releasing its place inside of me

Every time I sip tea

I feel poetry exploding

Waiting and wanting to ooze out of me

Oozing out in pleasured ecstasy filled phrases

Verbs making it orgasmically seductively

These are the words engulfed in me

Like the sip that invokes thoughts

As I feel the warm liquid running through my veins

Oh what a feeling

Sippin' tea...writing poetry

The Pain

Squeal the squealing

Silence the silent

Bury the buried

Who cares about the pain?

The one who squelches in mercy

Silenced through screams

Buried once

To die over and over again

Who carries the pain?

Who lifts the shattered pieces of the broken hearted?

Who shoulders the burden of rejection?

It's time to settle and sit in the uncertainty of it all

But does anyone truly care?

It's a matter of being aware

Holding it close to silence all pains

Squelch the scream

Knowing you are mountains of oceans

Tides of Tsunami

You are more than the pain

You are the power you possess inside

Attempted Murder

Attempted murder

Is the charge for the crime

The charge for not giving me time

Time to see the beauty inside of me

Grabbing the steel of shame

Loaded with bullets of self inflicted heartbreak

Hollow tips laced in unworthiness

Pointed at me in destruction

Aiming at the thoughts of not being enough

Firing at the judgment

Attempting to kill the joy inside of me

Murdering the chance of breathing life into one another

Shooting down the shots of laughter

Those moments of bliss

The feeling of ecstasy

Pulling the trigger

Killing the seeds that never grew

Killing what God created

This is not how it's supposed to end

I must remember who I am

The woman God created

The daughter he has protected

I vow to embrace all my sadness

My heartache

My pleasures

And all my joy

I vow not to forget the blissful ecstasy

Even in my time of pain

Cause I know this is all for me

It's my time to Live

To Thrive

To be the one and only

Poetic Yogi

The one created in divinity

Embracing my slow race

Breathing deeply

Feeling fully

Thankful the bullets missed me

Now I can thrive

In the life God purposed for me

Choose Me

In the face of adversity

In the eyes of guilt

In the body of shame

I choose me

I choose to keep the weight of my head held high

I choose to keep my sights right and aligned

Aligned with my purpose filled life

Today I choose the path that is least travel

While most protected

Traveling with my ancestors

Allowing my spirit to guide

And the creator to ground me

I choose me

My abilities and capabilities of being

Making a false man speak the truth

A wandering man seek truth

I am the chosen one

The one who chooses to spread truth

By shining my light internally

Today I choose the melody in my heart

The music in my soul

Today I choose to authentically and unapologetically be bold

Today I choose to be the woman God created me to be

I am the daughter he has protected

Unwrapping life's gifts he instilled in me

Today I choose the melody of my laugh

The whisper of my soul

Today I choose

The unapologetic...boldly motivated...fierce

Poetic Yogi

There Is You

There are men

Then there is you

There are people who hold the title of protector

Then there is you

It's you who has established the standard

The path of excellence

It's you who stood in the gap to bridge the weak to
stronger ground

Everyone has a smile

Then there's yours

A smile that twinkles in the dark

A laugh that's melody to the ear

You are the one

A rarity...a specialty...

There's some

There's few

There is only one incredible you

Lonely Love

Lonely love is still love

That love that makes your eyes dance at the sight of their smile

That kinda love making your ears melt at the sound of their name

That love that makes your tongue tingles with thoughts of their taste

That kinda love that makes your soul leap at the lifetime to be spent

But what happens when love is only one sided?

It becomes a lonely love

A love with no substance

Lacking the ability to create the art of love

A love you will cross an ocean for

But knowing they won't cross a puddle for you

How can you see someone's love for you?

When you want them to return it?

God made me to love the loveless

A light to shine in the darkness

A sweet something

In a world of sour nothings

Still love

Even when love is lonely

The Vow

Did you ever love me?

Did you know how to love you effectively?

Did you know how to love you effortlessly?

You vowed to adore me

Instead...

You began to ignore me

Ignoring the me you fell in love with

That teenage love

But at some point your love for me withered

Leaving my heart tattered and shattered

Vowing to protect me

But making the choice to neglect me

Decades of empty promises

Secrets never said

Betrayal of trust rooted in lies of lust

How could you?

Why would you hurt the one you love so effortlessly?

Using your tongue to slice my veins

Now you're dead and gone

I understand

You loved me from the place you knew

Loving me from the pain you grew from

When you met me

You felt a feeling you were unsure of

Feeling it was the answer from above

You gave it your all

The best way you knew how

I get it now

I forgive you

You loved me in the way you knew how

And I held on as long as I could

The boys are grown now

I had to grow to love me effortlessly

The way I'm purposed to

Vowing to love unconditionally

Without apology

Walking the path of serenity and clarity

Staying aligned as the one and only

POETIC YOGI

Beauty Defined

Black woman is Beauty Defined

Beauty of a black woman

An exquisite design

Created with patience and time

The Black woman is the epitome of spectacular

The whispers of knowledge

Sweetly soothing the voice of intuition

Soothing the loudest storm with words of honey

Gracious words sticking to the spirit

Healing for the soul

Defying odds with grace

Walking in feminine energy

The Black woman is everything there is

Everything there was

Everything that will ever be

The Black woman is why every man can be whoever they want to be

Her love is stronger than a tsunami

The Black woman is the standard

The Black woman IS the definition of Beauty

Good Grief

The lost of your heart is unexplainable

Wrapped in a blanket of uncertainty

Clothed in questions

The pain grabbing you

Spinning you

Tossing you

Hurling you into a sea of tears

Wallow of sadness

Yet seeing their smile in the midst of the tears

Hearing their laugh in the midst of your screams

Enjoying the hurt

Relished in love of the pain

At the loss of your love

Relished in the memories

Feeding the pain

Good grief...

Grief is a bitch

But necessary to remember life

Remembering the love

Releasing the anger in memorials

Showing passion in the loss of life

Through the creation of life

Allowing their life to live

Allowing their grief to have goodness

Shitty Motherfucker Era

If you let'em

People will dump their shit on you

Attempting to litter your presence with stench of
discontent

Laughing in your face

With the taste of gossip on their lips

Passively aggressively attacking the light they see

Cause their shade is too dark

Attempting to attack your peace

Lifting their leg up

Dumping their foul future

Their regretful past

Which ain't got shit to do with you

It's the way I allow them to be part of me

Detaching from all shady circumstances

Living the life of your dreams

Allowing folks to wallow in their filth

Refusing to let shit get in me or on me

If you let'em

People will dump shit all on you

Don't let'em

Release

The ability to release what no longer serves me is not easy

So many things be conditioned to know

Things we thought would help us grow

The things we hold on to so fiercely we have to let go

To walk into our God given ability

Releasing the people

Releasing things

Releasing circumstances that no longer serve us

Releasing the things that won't connect to what we're purposed to be

Releasing the things that no longer make our heart sing

Releasing what stops our joy

Releasing the bullshit to embrace the good shit

Life will throw things at you

Clouding the vision of who you are

Believing false narratives

Trapping us in a limited space

Staying in stagnancy

Limiting our abilities

Releasing the stagnancy

Finding grace in a space within

Finding love that permeates through you

Releasing what no longer serves to be the you

The YOU

Who you truly are

Love Jones Kinda Love

First sight kinda love

Makes you recite on sight

For the love of your life

A reflection of you

That Love Jones kinda love

Having you so deep in love

Making omelets and don't eat eggs kinda love

That Love Jones kinda love

Making you lose common sense

Letting your love go

Letting your love leave with no chance to recede the words

You didn't mean

That Love Jones kinda love

Got you chasing trains

The train that carries your heart

The train that holds your breath

The train that pulled off and took everything

Blues in my left thigh

Funk in my right

The Jones I have for you is darker than the starry night

Deeper than the deepest blue

You got me Jonesing for you

That Love Jones kinda love

The Loveless Love

Love defined feels good

Propelling you to the next level of life

Well...

I'm still searching for the real meaning

The true feeling of what love is

It has been such a fleeting feeling

I'm not sure if there will be a time I can enjoy love

Without feeling like I need to hold it tight

Let's define what love is

Is love the warmth of your hands holding a cup of tea?

Is love the excitement in the eye when you are seen?

Is love an opportunity to discover a new person?

For me...

Love is a bunch of bullshit

I've always tried to see the love in everything

But that shit is old now

I can't see it anymore

I haven't felt love in a looonnnggg time

Peole say they love me

But it feels like it's something said just to pass the time

Do they really love my weirdness?

Do they really understand my anger?

Do they love me at my core?

Is there a such thing as unconditional love?

What if everyone is trying to figure this shit out just like me?

No one seems to know what the hell love is

Or how it's supposed to operate

I guess I should take the moments given

No matter how fleeting they may be

Love Loss is you having love at one point to lose

I've searched for love for so long

Because I've never felt it

I knew my Grandma loved me without a shadow of a doubt with no conditions or attachments

She loved her some Bootsie

I didn't have to do anything

I didn't have to say anything

I didn't have to be any certain type of way

I just had to be me

And Grandma loved me unconditionally

That's the kinda love they don't make anymore

That Grandma love

The love you to the core type of love

Now she's gone

Where do I get that kinda love from?

Herschel

I knew that man love me more than himself

Because he couldn't love himself

So he poured all his love into me and those boys

Now he's gone

Can someone please tell me?

Where am I supposed to get love from?

Where am I supposed to feel included?

Who will ever give me a love that actually loves me?

It seems it will never be

Every time I think someone is down for me

I love them too hard and they run away

I'm sick of loving people that don't give a fuck about me

I'm sick of being there for motherfucker's that won't throw me a damn penny

What the hell

What the fuck for?

What's the purpose?

Why not just leave this fucking planet?

Folk just don't get it

They just don't understand how hard it is every day to not snap a motherfucker's neck

Breaking their spirit

Cracking their joy with words of venom

Not understanding how hard it is to hold back

That shit is old

And I'm ready to snap

Snapping people's neck who keep lying to me

Snapping necks of bitches trying me

Snapping the necks of niggas who think I'm a fucking joke

Going on a killing spree

Now everybody wanna ask questions

Bitch you know what happened

You know how you talked to me

You remember how you treated me

You're so full of shit

But I need to be that bitch

The one who used up a hoe without regard

I need to be that bitch

The one who don't give a fuck about another
motherfucker's feelings

Letting them have it

Blow for blow

Bitches just don't get it

I've kept this part of my life quiet

So I don't start a fucking riot

But you bitches and niggas keep trying me

You just don't know

You're gonna get the best bitch in me

You may have never seen her

But you need to get ready

Her performance will get a fucking Grammy

Because you hoes think I'm fucking playing with you

Thinking I'm nice all the time

But FUCK YOU BITCH

And the horse you rode in on too

All you Bitches ain't shit

Motherfucker's just don't know

How much you've been saved

That Bitch is put to bed

Bootsie in full blown

G's and D's mind led

Fuck you bitches

And you niggas too

It's a new day

Don't come over with the boo hoo hoo

I did enough of that shit

Just like you didn't have time for mine

I don't have time for yours

Making time for other's

When no one makes a second for me

I was a damn fool

But no more boo

Fuck you and that nigga too

I get it now

It just took me a minute

To actually make a move

But please believe

I will move long

Getting the hell away from you

Love

What the fuck is love?

Some are born with it

Some have never felt it

What is love?

A noun...

A verb...

A subject...

An adjective...

Will we ever know what love really is?

Is there a way to define something that defines itself?

How are we supposed to say we love you to the next
person if we aren't sure what love is?

Now this self love thing

I've been working on it for a minute

And to be honest

I still don't get it

I know I'm a bad ass no doubt

I feel that wholeheartedly

Deep inside of me

But does that mean I'm supposed to easily feel the love
the next motherfucker have for me?

I don't believe that shit

Get the fuck outta here

They can't love themselves

To a capacity to accept the love I give

So why in the hell do we buy into this self love bullshit?

When it's about self awareness

Knowing how you tick

Knowing how you act

Knowing how and what you do

Especially when you have that don't give a fuck attitude

Not giving a fuck what the next motherfucker has to say

So no I don't know what the fuck love is

Although I have a tattoo sitting on my wrist

Marketing that shit was trendy for me to do

This love thing is fleeting

I believe in joy

I believe in peace

I believe in happiness

This I can feel without questioning

But that love thing...

It leaves me to have too many questions

So I'll ask again...

What the fuck is love?

Think

T – Truth

H – Helpful

I – Intuitive

N – Necessary

K – Kind

Do you think before you speak?

Do your words hold truth?

Are they laced with intent of deceit?

Do you think about how you feel internally?

Do you speak intuitively?

Do you say what you think someone needs to hear?

Are your words necessary?

Invoking change

Providing solutions

Do you break down others without retribution?

Can your words ride the wave of love?

Do you speak things invoking suffering?

Enraging Silence

Are you kind?

For me...

I just say what's on my mind

You can take it or leave it

People don't care about the hurt attached to the verb

The verb laced in the subject

Saying what they think another motherfucker wants to hear

Taking what they say

Making it law

Trying to change how someone else moves and speaks

But guess what...

Let folks say what they will

They just talkin'

Their mouths are echoing in the echo of their speech

Those who shoot words of kindness laced in deceit

Are tough to navigate

That's when you count on how you feel

Hearing the "praise" words

Do you feel genuine love laced in the verbs?

Does it sound like envy in the volume the subject was said?

Listen to your gut

It will always let you know

If those speaking to you are against you

Are they really for you?

Or trying to stick it to you?

Remember...

Think before you speak

Ask yourself the questions

Become aware of the words you allow to leave your mind and exit your mouth

Once they leave the lips and hit the ears with intention

It's tough to gain back that trust

Switch that perception

Speak when you need to

God gave you one mouth and two ears for a reason

Listen to those around you without reason

Soak in the pleasure of their presence

Enjoy their essence

It's a gift you might not get again

So listen

Think

Me

It's a beautiful place to be **Me**

I finally gave myself permission to love **Me**

I know it may sound simple but let me tell you a story of a girl that didn't know how to love **Me**

She was born on the windy streets of Chi-Town

An only child to a mother with trauma

A father that doesn't want to be a father

A Grandma who stepped in and raised her Bootsie

From birth till my first born Herschel Jr.

Then my kid's father gave me the privilege of saying "I Do"

A husband and three more sons

That was our main focus

They were our pride and joy

Our boys gave us life

Then life happened

As they grew

Our love started to separate

And we didn't know what to do

Everything was surrounded around our boys

In 2016 I moved to Houston and he moved to Phoenix

In 2017 he found him a boo and I went to clear my head

It was time for me to find me

Being with one man since I was sixteen

Now I'm forty two

How in the hell do I navigate through this dating pool?

Who am I outside of my sons?

One more to raise

Who's about to spread his wings

What in the hell am I gonna do?

Who am I gonna be?

Especially without my guy

The one who's been by my side

Who is now on the other side of the country

I gotta figure this shit out

I started seeing through The Dirt

An outcome that could be brand new

2020 hit

And he was gone

Left his sons fatherless

Left us all clueless

The pain so deep

We have no place to put it

I lost not only my children's pops

I lost my best friend

Having to bury him

He wasn't even forty five

That shit was more than I wanted to do

Burying my boy was the last thing I thought I would have
to do

But acceptance is a hard pill to swallow

When all you know is rejection

Acceptance that a piece of your heart is gone

His death was a catalyst

Unburying the anger

Un-harboring the resentment

Setting an anchor in self awareness

I had to break my heart

Crack my spirit

Spilling my soul to uncover what was already whole

I had to see all the pain

The unworthiness game

The constant thoughts of what was not **Me**

I had to feel all the parts of the night with the light

Filling myself up consistently

Knowing the grandeur of my abilities

Walking in the path my ancestors have laid for me

Skipping in joy

For the abundance that has been righted to me

Grounded in the power of my feminine energy

The power of creation with Mother Earth

Life has cracked me wide open

But my smile spills brighter

When I was born to be the light of many

Walking in my path of ability

Love for me is a constant reminder of the love I have for many

But today I finally chose to love **Me**

Fuel

Negativity fuels some

But it drains me

How can negative energy give you the ability to be the
purposed being you were created to be?

Positive energy invokes the will to be the light

To be the positive charge

I guess sometimes you have to explore negative sight

To be able to appreciate the positive light

Fuel is defined as what makes us go

What keeps us moving in the flow

Fuel gives us the mode to push on

Giving us the strength to know we got this

Now is that fuel

More powerful

Negative or positive

The fuel type doesn't matter

As long as you are fueled with gas that ignites the fire in you

It's up to us to be what we were created to BEE

Happily Ever What?

Happily ever after

That's what every little girl dreams of

Believing that one day

Her knight will come save her in the darkest night

Thinking there will be true love

Making her a priority

Happily ever after

Seems to be just a dream

Especially for me

Being a teenage mother you marry your baby's father

Defying the statistics

Making sure your son has a black man in his life

A strong black father to guide him right

That's what our happily ever after consists of

Making sure our babies have the best life

My happily ever after wasn't about white picket fences

It was about making ends meet

While mending the fences

What is happily ever after to you?

I would like to believe we're deserving of some form of happiness

After all the bullshit

What does happily ever after look like?

Is it traveling through different countries?

Is it seeing the world in a different space than you grew to know?

What is happily ever after?

Is it for me to continue writing this fire ass poetry?

Creating pictures with my words?

Is being happy only after you live this life?

I mean really...

What is it?

Happily ever after

Never seems to find me

Happily I am

But ever after

I'm not sure about

After what?

After the pain?

After the drain?

After what?

Happily ever what?

Love and Heartbreak

If you don't love

You don't have heartbreak

The pain of the break hurts

But isn't worst to not have loved at all

Having the ability to fully love deeply

Open to be shattered repeatedly

Heart breaks aren't easy

But not feeling love isn't either

Is it worth the sacrifice of the heart?

To feel the fullness love can give

Broken hearts mean you loved

You once felt a love that was pure

Shattered hearts means you felt the pain of love

You felt the joy of the warmth of a smile

Inflating your heart

Floating through life on love

The love that breaks you

Is the love that keeps you

Is it better to not feel the warmth?

To never feel the love

So the heart is never breaking

Love Question

I am loved

But is it true?

Does the love I wish to feel come from a boo?

When is it true?

What makes me know the action of love is verbing?

How do I know it's not swerving?

The question of love is one that has many answers

Multiple choices to choose from

Yet feeling like the answer is more false than true

With a lot to lose

Losing a piece of my heart is a fight I keep getting defeated

The heart is tense

Tired of these false intentions

I love you they say

But what condition is laced with this statement?

What did I do?

What do I need to do?

For this love to feel safe...seen...and understood

That the thing about love

There's nothing needed

There's no conditions required for it to be true

It's the love you have for you

The love I have for me

Looking outside myself for a lifetime of love

Crying many times

When I wasn't included

Thinking I had to do something to get folks to love me

But that didn't work

Everyone has their own capacity of love

Some is overflowing

Giving the ability to love completely

When some have a half cup of love

Barely having enough for them to get through

Love is an art

Intentionally crafted for you

It's about self awareness

Knowing how to genuinely love you

Random

Thoughts...questions...suggestions

Hold real estate in my mind

It's time for the contract to rescind

Allowing me to go within

Recognizing the thoughts of judgment

Acts of betrayal

Fears of abandonment

Not speaking my truth

Thinking it will make them stay

Creating a tsunami of feelings engulfed

Tears strangling me in my sadness

My aching heart hollows

Old...

Bored...

Not seen...

Not needed...

Here for a moment...

Here for a time...

To do what?

To connect with another heart

Seeing another soul unseen

Feelings of unworthiness

Wondering why no one has chosen me

Why doesn't anyone want to genuinely love me?

Have I done something to be unworthy?

Unworthy of a deserving love

What has happened?

Why won't the companion for me appear to me?

I was in a marriage

With a man who didn't have the capacity to love me

I'm the person who loves love

But am I missing it?

I seriously doubt it

I just don't feel it

Sad and lonely most nights

Singly crying

When I can't take no more

Aching for the hug

Wishing for a kiss

Wanting to watch TV with my head in his lap

Hands wrapped around me

Just for a moment

The things we take for granted

When they're not there anymore

We might have been equally yoked

But we were there without regard

Listening to each other

Seeing one another

That's why God put us together

But don't worry about me

I'm just speaking randomly

With my random thoughts

The ones holding real estate in my mind

If Only

If only

I could bring them back

If only

I could say that one thing to make them stay

If only

I could make them see

What if it wasn't for me to say?

To do

To only be

Thoughts of guilt weigh in the air

Thicker than braided hair

The guilt of If Only

The weight of What If

Is too much to bear

It's time to let it go

We can't hold on to what was

What I thought could be

It's time to see what is

What's in front of me

Seeing the love my four sons give unconditionally

Feeling the power

The joy they hold

The wound of rejection salting my eyes

Burning views of doubt

The wound of abandonment

Oozing self sabotage

The salve of healing

Unconditional love

To care from within me

The little girl within me

Has been crying for so long

Screaming...

SEE ME!

I see you baby girl

I hear you

I protect you

If Only

Integrating what was

Walking in the now of what is

Being in the now

Is all I can and will ever be!

Trapping Fear-ode to Trap City Café

Trapped in a city

Filled with lies

Full of fear

Tip the King for creating a city that fear can not lie

The city shines

Fear is a lie

Fear is false evidence appearing real

A lie told to not be in reality

Choosing fear chooses suffering

Choosing to not be wonderfully made

Fear grabbing hold of your spirit

Stalling your steps to the purposed path

Holding on to fear is holding on to wrath

Clouding the way with debris of lies and discontent

Fear is a lie

Don't get trapped in a city of self

Where fear lives and lies

Stench of Unworthiness

I've been a desperate love seeking...wound dripping mess
for way too long

Allowing the pain of others to seep into the existence of
my energy

Convinced I wasn't worthy of anything

Begging for attention

From those who aren't attentive to themselves

How in the hell did I ever think they were the one to make
me?

When I was created by the one and only

G O D

But my fears and insecurities had me thinking

I needed man to justify me

That was my hard pill to swallow

Knowing

I put myself in those dark places with people

Allowing them to waste my energy

But was it really a waste?

Let me rephrase it

I was placed where I need to be

To inner stand where I ought to be

Feeling the rejection of abandonment

Learning to no longer abandon me

No more rejecting me

Inner standing how to fully trust...respect...and be loyal to
ME

Nineteen with two kids

I didn't understand the plan God had for me

I didn't know I was worthy

I had to fly through a windshield and crack my skull open

To close the wound twenty years later

For me to tell you this...

Life is more than today

Learn from today

To enjoy tomorrow

Don't stay in yesterday

Live now in the present

It's a gift

Missing Choc

Silence is loud

No longer hearing your laughter

Cries muffled

Stopping the screams

Heartbreaks at the seams

The pain is real

This is true

That Dixon legacy is what you created

These four handsome men take after you

Their hustle...ambition...and drive

No nonsense involved

The discipline in you instilled in them

Now they inspire in others

Being the men you raised them to be

We miss you Choc

Bath Time

A time to cleanse and release

All that's not for me

Moments of peace

Drowning in gratefulness

Becoming everything I'm purposed to be

Soak without jokes

Bathe to release the shade

Creating a space of pleasure

Embracing and exploring every inch of me

Burning sage for clearing

Two candles for clarity

Seeing the power within me

A few cups of sea salt

Removing all the negative energy

A few drops of lavender

Welcoming serenity

Draining fears wrapped in doubt

Washing the tide of pride

It's Chocolate Honey Bath Time

Black Love

My Black Man

You are royalty

Hands strong enough to hold me

Holding my heart

You & Me

We are meant to be

We are the essence of what our ancestors dreamt we
would be

Loving each other openly

Intentionally and genuinely

This love we share is one that will pass down to
generations

Ten times...ten fold

Black Love is you the Black Man and Me the Black Woman

We are purposed to be

Expectations

Do you dream of having a relationship?

Where love knows the conditions you require

Do you wish for a relationship?

Where expectations are understood

And the expected results always deliver

Maybe you want an engagement or entanglement without judgment

Well...you can keep all three

I'm not living in conditional mode

Where expectations are never known

Ending with judgment

Leaving your heart shattered

Asking why

Conditional expectations

Wrapped self imposed stories

Laced with lies of protection

Is not where I want love to go

This love needs to flow

Flowing into the space of the heart of the one

The one who fill the gaps of lies

The holes of resentment

Gutters of deceit

The love from the one

Will be a heaven sent type of love

Coming to tighten the corners of my eyes

Decreasing the soul cries

Ready to receive love of the one

The one who was created to feel to be with me in truth

Patiently waiting what's for me

Releasing the need to control the outcome

Relinquishing the power to God that flows in me

Everything happens as it should

There's nothing more for me to do

I'm only required to live in the realms of dreams

Creating visions through imagination

Of unlimited possibilities

My expectation is for me to be committed

Committed to the relationship with me

Expectations to give me what I need

Being the purposed being daily

The Little Girl

Entertaining the wrong kind

Can put you in a flurry mind

State of anxious confusion

False thoughts of love

Intrusive stake in my heart of common sense

Delusion theories laced with false reunions and family adoptions

The thought of being one with anyone but ME

Searching for the little girl lost

Telling her she's no longer lost

We're standing as one

Just me and the little girl in me

Do It

Have you ever done something that scares you and excites you at the same time?

Have you ever answered the call to your wildest desires?

Once you answer

The spirit is awakened

The soul is soothed

When the answer of purpose is resolved

Resolved in knowing your role is bigger than you

Knowing your assignment

This desire

The desire GOD put it in your heart

That's the purposed part

The part you do what excites you and scares you at the same time

Just DO IT!

Illusionary Tale

The illusion of we is what my heart wants to feel

The illusion of we is what my mind wants to see

The truth is...

There is no we

There is you doing your thang over there

There is me doing me over here

Talking to each other sometimes

A lot of we moments

Taken into an illusionary tale

That means you and me

But not like that anyways

It's a conversation between friends

That's the WE that WE are

Just two friends chatting

It isn't the more my heart wants to feel

It's not the WE my mind translates it to be

This illusion of WE is laced with my insecurities

Abandonment wrapped with a needy glow

The illusion of the WE I want to see

The one that love speaks loud for me

Creating time

Knowing I am yours and you are mine

We're all that matters

Blocking the world from the outside

Just you and me flowing happily

Sitting on the porch

Sipping tea in different countries

But these illusionary tales seem delusional

Thinking you genuinely wanted to love me

But that's not the person you want to be

This is a fact I must keep in tact

Reminding my mind of the love I give

It's one of a kind

A love without conditions

Requiring no expectations

Given to those who want to receive it

I know you're not feeling me as your boo

And that's cool

I still got mad love for you

But now it's time for me to wake up

Wake up out of this illusionary state

Stop taking the bait

Of living in this illusionary tale

Celebrate

Time to meditate on the best way to celebrate

Celebrating the choice I made to finally choose me

Time to ooze of gratitude overflowing

God's blessings reigning over me

Time to sit and marvel in the power

As my world travels the hearts of purposed to hear

To the souls awaken to answer the call

Time to rise in the confident Queendom energy

God created me to be

Time to celebrate the power

The power within me

Yogatry

Yogatry

The ability to create the infusion of me

Releasing the doubt of unworthiness

Embracing a spirit of creativity

Placing my heart in a space to break down wall of scarcity

Shattering the energy of lack

Instead...

Learning to love the dark parts

The hidden thoughts

The joy of my shine

The light of my suns

The belief of making dreams a reality

Unleashing a different part of me

Honey Yogatry

A suppressed expression

Waiting to release the creativity

Laced with spontaneity

The reveal is real

Sprouting the seeds of thought

Into a space of healing

For the one who takes the journey to travel

Honey Yogatry

Sweet yoga

Poetic healing

Your sacred space

To just BEE

That Love

That love

That makes you dance...shake...and embrace

That love

That sits in your lap

Heart to heart

Head to head

Filling each other up with power

Power of the breath of life

Intentionally meditation the beats of the heart

1...2...3...It's me

1...2...3...It's you

It's that love

Bowl of Cereal

Dip your spoon into this sweet warm cavity

Explore inside

Discovering the prize

Feeling the honey nut

Ooohhh ooohhh

Mmmmm...mmmmm...

Don't stop filling my Cheerios

Using my body as your spoon

Taking me in and out

Out and in

Between your lips

Marinating in your mouth

Lick me

Eat me

Suck me

Don't miss a drop

With tonguing precision

Eat me like a bowl of cereal

Wrapping your tongue in the Cheerio hole

Savor me

Devour me

Delight me

Enjoy every taste of me

Like a bowl of Reese's Puff and Honey Nut Cheerios

The perfect combo

Chocolate Honey

About The Author

The Poetic Yogi speaks words of honey—her voice a bridge between wisdom and wonder, truth and transformation. A seeker of life's sweetness, she has spent over 25 years guiding others toward secure futures in the retirement industry, yet the last decade has been a journey inward—unraveling the present through breath, movement, and the alchemy of emotion.

As a certified yoga instructor, meditation guide, and award-winning spoken word artist, she weaves the tangible with the unseen, turning experience into verse and silence into story. She is the visionary behind **Honey Yogatry**, a holistic sanctuary where yoga, poetry, meditation, breathwork, and the healing energy of nature come together to uncover the depths of the soul.

Her work—whether spoken, written, or embodied—is more than art; it is rhythm, revelation, and restoration. It invites the reader, the listener, and the seeker into a space of transformation, exploring heartbreak and healing, love and loss, fear and freedom.

A proud mother of four sons and a beloved fur baby, she currently resides in Chicago, Illinois, with deep roots in Houston and Atlanta. She finds joy in traveling, poetry, reading, and dancing—embracing life's poetry in motion.

Made in the USA
Columbia, SC
25 July 2025

61030057R00076